A Benjamin Blog
and his Inquisitive Dog
Investigation

Exploring
Mountains

Anita Ganeri

raintree
a Capstone company — publishers for children

Raintree is an imprint of Capstone Global Library Limited, a company incorporated in England and Wales having its registered office at 7 Pilgrim Street, London, EC4V 6LB – Registered company number: 6695582

www.raintreepublishers.co.uk
myorders@raintreepublishers.co.uk

Text © Capstone Global Library Limited 2014
First published in hardback in 2014
Paperback edition first published in 2015
The moral rights of the proprietor have been asserted.

Edited by Dan Nunn, Rebecca Rissman, and Helen Cox-Cannons
Designed by Joanna Hinton-Malivoire
Original illustrations © Capstone Global Library Ltd
Illustrated by Sernur ISIK
Picture research by Mica Brancic
Originated by Capstone Global Library Ltd
Production by Helen McCreath
Printed and bound in China

ISBN 978 1 406 27104 1 (hardback)
17 16 15 14 13
10 9 8 7 6 5 4 3 2 1

ISBN 978 1 406 27111 9 (paperback)
18 17 16 15 14
10 9 8 7 6 5 4 3 2 1

British Library Cataloguing in Publication Data
A full catalogue record for this book is available from the British Library.

Acknowledgements
We would like to thank the following for permission to reproduce photographs: Alamy p. 15 (Mountain Light/© Galen Rowell); Getty Images pp. 5 (Raja Islam), 8 (Photodisc/Stuart Dee), 10 (Aurora/Johnathan Ampersand Esper), 22 (Nigel Pavitt), 25 (Time Life Pictures/James Burke), 26 (AFP/Namgyal Sherpa); Shutterstock pp. 6 (© mikenorton), 12 (© pinggr), 14 (© Pablo H Caridad), 17 (© Mariusz Niedzwiedzki), 18 (© Josh Schutz), 19 (© Ammit Jack), 20 (© Krom1975), 21 (© Arsgera), 23 (© Ian Woolcock), 24 (© Vixit), 27 (© Ian Woolcock), 29 top (© Roberto Cerruti), 29 bottom (© BG Smith); SuperStock pp. 4 (National Geographic/Beth Wald), 7 (Design Pics/Axiom Photographic), 9 (age fotostock), 11 (All Canada Photos/Claude Robidoux), 13 (imagebroker.net), 16 (F1 ONLINE).

Front cover photograph of a mountain landscape reproduced with permission of Shutterstock (© Pichugin Dmitry).

We would like to thank Michael Bright for his invaluable help in the preparation of this book.

Every effort has been made to contact copyright holders of material reproduced in this book. Any omissions will be rectified in subsequent printings if notice is given to the publisher.

Disclaimer
All the internet addresses (URLs) given in this book were valid at the time of going to press. However, due to the dynamic nature of the internet, some addresses may have changed, or sites may have changed or ceased to exist since publication. While the author and publisher regret any inconvenience this may cause readers, no responsibility for any such changes can be accepted by either the author or the publisher.

Some words are shown in bold, **like this**. You can find out what they mean by looking in the glossary.

Contents

Welcome to the mountains!

Hello! My name's Benjamin Blog and this is Barko Polo, my **inquisitive** dog. (He's named after the ancient ace explorer **Marco Polo**.) We have just got back from our latest adventure – exploring mountains around the world. We put this book together from some of the blog posts we wrote on the way.

BARKO'S BLOG-TASTIC MOUNTAIN FACTS

Mountains are roughly more than 1,000 metres (3,333 feet) high above their surrounding area. Some are much higher – a mountain called K2, between Pakistan and China, is 8,611 metres (28,251 feet) tall – lucky I'm not scared of heights!

Mountain making

Posted by: Ben Blog | 20 December at 8.35 a.m.

The first stop on our trip was the Rocky Mountains in the United States. The Rockies are fold mountains. They were formed millions of years ago when two giant slabs of Earth's **crust** crashed into each other. This pushed the land in between upwards into giant folds.

BARKO'S BLOG-TASTIC MOUNTAIN FACTS

The Himalayas in Asia are the highest mountains on Earth. They were gradually formed after India crashed into the rest of Asia about 50 million years ago. What a sight!

Giant blocks and red-hot rocks

Posted by: Ben Blog | 25 December at 12.00 p.m.

From the Rockies, we headed across to Canada, where Barko took this photo of me in front of Mount Rundle. Mount Rundle is a block mountain. It was formed from a massive block of rock that got pushed up between two cracks in Earth's **crust**.

BARKO'S BLOG-TASTIC MOUNTAIN FACTS

Volcanoes happen when red-hot rock from deep underground comes up through cracks in Earth's crust. This is Cotopaxi in Ecuador. It hasn't **erupted** for 70 years, but I'm not going any closer, just in case!

Blowing a gale

Posted by: Ben Blog | 14 January at 3.16 p.m.

We are on the **summit** of Mount Kilimanjaro in Africa, and it's blowing a gale and freezing cold. The higher up a mountain you go, the colder it gets. That's why you get ice and snow on the top of Kilimanjaro, even though it's near the steamy **equator**.

BARKO'S BLOG-TASTIC MOUNTAIN FACTS

A blizzard is a violent snow storm that can blow up without warning. The wind blasts the snow into your face, so it's difficult to breathe or see anything. Who's there?

Knocked into shape

We arrived in the Alps this morning and headed straight for the Matterhorn on the border between Italy and Switzerland. Here's one of the photos I took. Over millions of years, the wind, water, and changes in temperature have worn the mountain into its jagged shape.

BARKO'S BLOG-TASTIC MOUNTAIN FACTS

This flat-topped mountain is near Cape Town in South Africa. It is 1,085 metres (3,559 feet) high. The wind and rain have worn it into a shape like a table. Can you guess what it's called?

Flowing ice, falling snow

Posted by: Ben Blog | 17 March at 4.00 p.m.

Glaciers are like gigantic rivers of ice that flow slowly down some mountain slopes. As they flow, they drag along rocks and boulders that scrape out U-shaped valleys in the mountainsides. This is the Perito Moreno glacier in Argentina. It's awesome.

BARKO'S BLOG-TASTIC MOUNTAIN FACTS

An **avalanche** is when thousands of tonnes of snow suddenly crash at high speed down a mountain. The snow buries everything in its way – trees, cars, houses, and people.

Living the high life

Posted by: Ben Blog | 2 April at 9.18 a.m.

Animals need to be tough to live on a mountain. They have to cope with the cold, wind, snow, and steep slopes. I snapped this yak high up in the Himalayas, where it's bitterly cold. Luckily, yaks have very long, shaggy coats to keep them warm.

BARKO'S BLOG-TASTIC MOUNTAIN FACTS
Marmots in the Alps survive the winter by **hibernating** in burrows underground. They wake up again in spring, when it's warmer and there is more food around. Yawn!

We came across these mountain goats while we were scrambling about in the Rocky Mountains. They're brilliant at climbing, even if the slopes are very steep. Their hooves have sharp edges for digging into cracks in the rocks and pads that stop them from slipping.

BARKO'S BLOG-TASTIC MOUNTAIN FACTS

Andean condors are massive birds that soar above the slopes of the Andes Mountains in South America. They have huge wings for gliding on gusts of wind.

Sprouting slopes

Posted by: Ben Blog | 10 July at 1.00 p.m.

In summer, we headed back to the Alps to search for edelweiss. These tiny mountain plants have cleverly adapted to the cold and windy conditions. The first thing you notice about them is their furry leaves. These trap heat from the Sun and stop precious water being lost.

BARKO'S BLOG-TASTIC MOUNTAIN FACTS

High up on a mountain, you can see a treeline, or a line where trees stop growing. Above the treeline, it's too cold and windy for trees to grow.

treeline

I snapped this amazing plant in the Aberdare Mountains of Kenya, in Africa. Most mountain plants grow low to the ground to keep out of the wind, but not this giant groundsel. Giant groundsels can reach 10 metres (33 feet) high – that's about six times as tall as me.

BARKO'S BLOG-TASTIC MOUNTAIN FACTS

The splashes of colour on these rocks are tiny plant-like living things, called **lichen**. They make **acids** that **dissolve** the rocks. The lichen dig their hair-like roots into the cracks to fix themselves to the rocks.

High-rise Everest

Posted by: Ben Blog | 27 September at 6.00 a.m.

Back in the Himalayas, we are getting ready to climb Mount Everest – the highlight of our trip. It won't be easy. Mount Everest is the highest mountain on Earth – it's 8,850 metres (29,035 feet) tall. It takes several days to climb from **base camp** to the **summit**. Wish us luck!

BARKO'S BLOG-TASTIC MOUNTAN FACTS
The first people to climb Mount Everest were Edmund Hillary from New Zealand and Tenzing Norgay from Nepal. They reached the summit on 29 May 1953.

Mountains of rubbish

Posted by: Ben Blog | 2 October at 4.19 p.m.

We made it! Now it's back to **base camp** to pack up and do a quick litter pick. Mountains are brilliant places for climbing, skiing, hiking, rafting, and **paragliding**. But people are leaving tonnes of rubbish behind, and it's making a terrible mess.

BARKO'S BLOG-TASTIC MOUNTAIN FACTS

Many mountain ranges have been made into national parks to protect them. You can see these amazing rocks in the Blue Mountains National Park in Australia. Legend says that they were once three sisters who were turned into stone.

Mighty mountains quiz

If you are planning your own mountain expedition, you need to be prepared. Find out how much you know about mighty mountains with our quick quiz.

1. What type of mountains are the Rockies?
a) fold
b) block
c) dome

2. What happens to the temperature the higher up you go?
a) it gets warmer
b) it gets colder
c) it stays the same

3. What is a **glacier**?
a) a sudden fall of snow
b) a type of mountain
c) a river of ice

4. How do yaks keep warm?
a) they **hibernate**
b) they have thick fur coats
c) they stay indoors

5. How do **lichens** break up rocks?
a) using acid
b) using hammers
c) using other rocks

6. Which is the world's highest mountain?
a) Everest
b) Kilimanjaro
c) K2

7. What is this?

8. What is this?

Glossary

acid liquid that breaks down rocks and other materials

avalanche sudden, massive fall of snow on a mountainside

base camp camp at the bottom of a mountain where climbers begin their climb

crust outer, rocky surface of Earth

dissolve turn something solid into liquid

equator imaginary line that runs around the middle of Earth

erupt when red-hot rock from underground comes up through cracks in Earth's crust

glacier huge river of ice that flows down a mountainside

hibernating sleeping during the winter when it is cold and there is little food about

inquisitive interested in learning about the world

lichen tiny plant-like living things that grow in crusty or bushy patches on trees and rocks

Marco Polo explorer who lived from about 1254 to 1324. He travelled from Italy to China.

paragliding sport where a person glides through the air, hanging from a wing-shaped parachute

summit top of a mountain

Find out more

Books

100 Things You Should Know about Extreme Earth, Belinda Gallagher (Miles Kelly, 2009)

Harsh Habitats (Extreme Nature), Anita Ganeri (Raintree, 2013)

Mountains (Science Kids), Margaret Hynes (Kingfisher, 2009)

The World's Most Amazing Mountains, Anna Clayborne (Raintree, 2009)

Websites

environment.nationalgeographic.com/ environment/habitats
This National Geographic website covers a range of habitats.

www.bbc.co.uk/bitesize/ks2/science/living_ things/plant_animal_habitats/read/1
Learn about habitats on this BBC website.

Index